WALKS AROU...
AMBLESIDE

10 WALKS UNDER 6 MILES

Dalesman

First published in 1997 by Dalesman
an imprint of
Country Publications Ltd
The Water Mill, Broughton Hall
Skipton, North Yorkshire BD23 3AG

Reprinted 1998, 1999, 2002, 2003, 2005, 2007, 2008

Text © Tom Bowker 1997
Maps © Jeremy Ashcroft 1997
Illustrations © Christine Isherwood 1997: p4, orange-tip butterfly; p7,
High Sweden Bridge; p11, dipper; p15, great burnet, wood cranesbill
and hay rattle; p20, purple loosestrife; p22, Skelwith Force; p25, red
squirrel; p27, treecreeper; p31, Blea Tarn and Langdale Pikes

Cover: Ambleside from Todd Crag by Julie Fryer

A British Library Cataloguing-in-Publication record
is available for this book

ISBN: 978-1-85568-117-0

Contents

Introduction

This book is aimed primarily at the modest walker, the holiday-maker or the family party, who would probably only attempt these walks in fine and clear weather. It is expected that some kind of pack will be carried, containing food, drink, a spare sweater, and waterproof/windproof clothing of some type, with the addition of gloves and a hat in winter. I strongly advise boots or stoutly-soled walking shoes.

All the walks described are on official rights-of-way, permissive footpaths or public access areas and are as up-to-date as possible. Paths can change from time to time, in which case there should be a signpost specifically indicating any alteration.

Ambleside, and Waterhead its "port", have much of interest to offer other than their beautiful surroundings. There are ancient buildings, many of literary as well as architectural interest, lovely parks and playgrounds, a garden centre, cinema, youth hostel, and a wide variety of shops, restaurants, cafes and pubs. Painters, glass-blowers, photographers and other craftsmen have studios and can be seen at work here.

A short car or bus journey away, Troutbeck offers lovely walks and lovingly restored traditional dwellings. Great Langdale and Little Langdale offer the modest walker a taste of wild mountain Lakeland.

In the walks described, peaks are "bagged", woods, waterfalls, tarns and old quarries explored, with many a lovely impromptu picnic spot revealed. Just get out there and let Lakeland soak into your soul.

Happy walking!

Stock Ghyll Force

Length of Walk: 3 miles.
Start/finish: In Ambleside, by the steps of the old Market Cross, which is no longer surmounted by a cross, near the pedestrian crossing at the junction of North Road and the A591.
Terrain: A climb alongside lovely waterfalls is followed by pleasurable walking along easy paths and farm tracks.

Cross North Road and walk up the A591 to where it bends right. Turn left, along the alleyway between Barclays Bank and the Market Hall into Cheapside. Turn left, passing between a "Waterfalls" sign and a "Stock Ghyll Wansfell Pike" sign. Climb Stock Ghyll Lane to where a metal gateway, on the left, leads into Stock Ghyll Park.

Follow the red waymarker arrows until you meet a left and right one. Turn left across a footbridge over the beck and climb up the left bank to a fenced path forking right. It's a dead-end but gives a splendid view of the falls, especially if they are in spate. Return to the upper path and climb right to reach and cross a footbridge above the falls. Turn right, past a picnic table, then steeply down to another picnic table. Turn left here, away from the falls, along a path (arrowed) heading through an old turnstile-gate in a wall. The turnstile is a relic of the days when the falls were privately owned and only seen on payment of a fee.

Turn left up the Tarmac strip, signposted "Public Footpath". Beyond a cattle grid, look left to see the Langdale Pikes. Many Lakeland place-names are derived from the Norsemen (Vikings) who settled peaceably here in the 10th century. Political refugees, apparently, fleeing from settlements in Ireland, not pillagers and plunderers. Langdale means "long valley" and "pike" a sharp summit. The dominant fell ahead is Red Screes, which takes its name from the sanguine rocks of the corrie which can be seen hanging below its summit and above the Kirkstone Pass Inn. Far to the right of the inn is flattish, pimple-crowned Thornthwaite Crag. The "pimple" is an elegant, chimney-like cairn some 20ft high.

Climb on, passing by a stile signposted "Troutbeck via Wansfell", to eventually reach Low Grove House, where the Tarmac bridges a beck. Cross

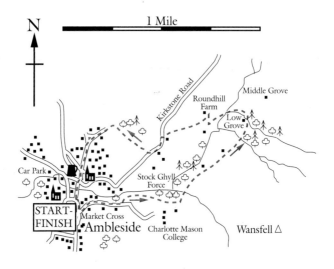

a cattle-grid and turn left, off the Tarmac, following a yellow waymarker arrow, through a gap in the hedge-line, into a field. Go down to and across a footbridge over the Stock Ghyll. Walk left, then zig-zag up to a gate leading onto Roundhill Farm track. Turn left, ("Footpath" sign opposite), along the rough track to join Kirkstone Road. Wansfell looms across the valley to your left. Windermere gleams below and ahead, with flattish Latterbarrow, above Hawkshead, and wooded Claife Heights rising beyond.

Turn left down Kirkstone Road to a "Public Footpath/Ellerigg" sign pointing right. Follow this path to shortly reach a memorial bench overlooking Ambleside. From here, the Parish Church, built between 1850 and 1854, dominates Ambleside's rooftops. Walk on. Beyond a "Dogs on Leads" gate, the path crosses a field then climbs a stone stile crowned by a tiny metal gate. Go down and across the field beyond to cross a "clapper bridge" (a slab of rock laid over a beck or ditch), and another gated stone stile. Walk along the driveway beyond to emerge onto Ellerigg Road. Turn left down the road to shortly join Sweden Bridge Lane and so down to Ambleside. From this junction you could, if you are feeling fit, continue along Walk 2.

High Sweden Bridge

Length of walk: 3 miles.
Start/finish: In Ambleside, by the steps of the old Market Cross, which is no longer surmounted by a cross, near the pedestrian crossing at the junction of North Road and the A591.
Terrain: A steady climb to High Sweden Bridge and a ridge viewpoint, on good paths throughout. Then it's downhill all the way.

Turn left along North Road to its junction with Smithy Brow. Climb steeply right to shortly turn left up Sweden Bridge Lane. Climb on, ignoring Belle Vue Lane, to the junction with Ellerigg Road, where fit Walk 1 walkers could link up with Walk 2. Climb onwards, to a gate leading into a narrow, stony, walled path. As you climb the path widens, as does your view to the left. (To be described in detail from the walk's high point.) Rydal Water, probably the Wordsworths' most loved lake, gleams below.

Eventually, after passing through a gate, the path becomes wooded with the ground to your left falling steeply away into rocky, cascading Scandale Beck. Slate quarrying, possibly the most ancient of Lakeland crafts, for the roofs of Galava, Ambleside's Roman fort were slated, is evident in dark, damp holes passed in the trees to your right. Small, derelict quarries like these, used for local needs, are scattered all over Lakeland, inexorably greening and harmonising into the natural beauty of the fells, and becoming a haven for wild flowers and nesting birds. Your path crosses the "spoil heap", the dump of waste slate extracted and extending over the beck.

When the path emerges from the trees, it forks. Walk left, alongside the beck, to High Sweden Bridge, "a timeless piece of vernacular architecture". A true

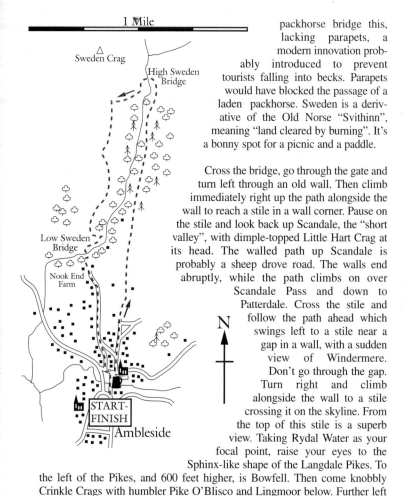

1 Mile

Sweden Crag

High Sweden Bridge

Low Sweden Bridge

Nook End Farm

START-FINISH

Ambleside

N

packhorse bridge this, lacking parapets, a modern innovation probably introduced to prevent tourists falling into becks. Parapets would have blocked the passage of a laden packhorse. Sweden is a derivative of the Old Norse "Svithinn", meaning "land cleared by burning". It's a bonny spot for a picnic and a paddle.

Cross the bridge, go through the gate and turn left through an old wall. Then climb immediately right up the path alongside the wall to reach a stile in a wall corner. Pause on the stile and look back up Scandale, the "short valley", with dimple-topped Little Hart Crag at its head. The walled path up Scandale is probably a sheep drove road. The walls end abruptly, while the path climbs on over Scandale Pass and down to Patterdale. Cross the stile and follow the path ahead which swings left to a stile near a gap in a wall, with a sudden view of Windermere. Don't go through the gap. Turn right and climb alongside the wall to a stile crossing it on the skyline. From the top of this stile is a superb view. Taking Rydal Water as your focal point, raise your eyes to the Sphinx-like shape of the Langdale Pikes. To the left of the Pikes, and 600 feet higher, is Bowfell. Then come knobbly Crinkle Crags with humbler Pike O'Blisco and Lingmoor below. Further left is Wrynose Pass, Wetherlam and Coniston Old Man.

Cross the stile and follow the good path down the ridge, passing through wall gaps and past redundant stiles, to eventually swing left and across Low Sweden Bridge and up through the yard of Nook End Farm. Follow Nook Lane back down into Ambleside.

Rydal Cave

Length of walk: 5 miles.
Start/finish: In Ambleside, by the steps of the old Market Cross, which is no longer surmounted by a cross, near the pedestrian crossing at the junction of North Road and the A591.
Terrain: A steepish climb early on, followed by brackeny, sometimes squishy paths, then quarry-caves, lakeside paths and parkland.

Cross the pedestrian crossing, turn right, then left down Compston Road. Turn right at the cinema, then immediately left, signposted "Rothay Park/ Loughrigg", into Vicarage Road and on past the Parish Church. Built between 1850-1854, it features a lovely mural of the traditional Lakeland rushbearing ceremony. Walk through Rothay Park. Todd Crag looms above, whilst the huge, lumpy armchair of fells, to your right, is the Fairfield Horseshoe. Cross the Rothay by a humpbacked bridge onto a minor road. Turn right, over a cattle grid, then left, over another cattle grid, signposted "Public Bridleway". Climb the twisting Tarmac strip beyond to a "Public Footpath/Clappersgate" sign. Climb left over a stile, along a narrow path, through a gap, and over a beck onto the open fellside and a junction of paths.

Turn right, up steps (arrowed), then right again, looking for another path forking left across the fellside. Turn left along this, passing below a rocky, tree-clad hummock. Eventually, you emerge onto a top crowned by a cairn (pile of stones) and the end of a wall. Climb on a little way, crossing a stile over a wall, to reach two rocky tops, divided by a gap, either of which is arguably the summit of Todd Crag (695 feet).

The "birds eye" view over Windermere is breathtaking. My eyes always wander, however, to the ruins of "Galava", the Roman fort, on its promontory by the mouth of the Rothay. This design of fort remained unchanged for centuries and was built on conquered soil from Perthshire to Palestine. Roman sentinels must have looked up and seen a Brigante war-party poised, like Apaches in a John Wayne film, upon the very rocks on which you are standing.

In the gap between the highest tops, turn your back on Windermere. Go down, over, and to the left of a tiny tarn (sometimes dried up). Over again, then down to the right of larger Lily Tarn.

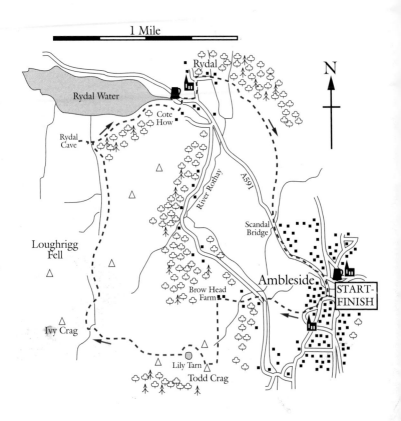

Now comes the tricky bit, for the fell hereabouts is dimpled with hummocks and criss-crossed with paths. Follow the path, ignoring all other paths, and be aware that you are following a wall, away over to your left. Soon your path veers alongside this wall to meet a crossing fence. Go through the gate and continue with the wall, again ignoring all other paths, descending to the left of a hummock. When approaching a beck spilling leftwards, the wall turns down and away. You follow your path which crosses the beck and climbs right to join a wider, eroded crossing path. Turn right, along this path, to shortly cross back over the beck, then, almost immediately, turn left along a narrow path through the bracken. Again, ignore all other paths as you climb towards a flattish-topped hummock. At a T-junction of paths, however, turn left and follow this path to eventually climb into a gap crowned by a cairn.

It's straightforward going now, down the path beyond the cairn to shortly see Rydal Water below, and the cocky cone of Helm Crag, also known as The Lion and the Lamb, above unseen Grasmere. Eventually, you join a wider, firmer crossing path where it bridges a beck. Climb left, passing a quarry/cave guarded by a rocky pinnacle, to shortly reach the huge, derelict quarry/cave known as Rydal Cave. If you're a photographer, go inside and look out for the dramatic view of the jagged black archway curving over entrance pool and trees, far fellside and their reflections. It's a shot that will make your friends gasp.

Retrace your steps past the lower cave, and follow the path down until the wall on your left turns away. Now turn steeply left down the grassy bank, passing a seat, to the water's edge. Turn right through a metal gate in a wall and on through Rydal Woods to a footbridge over the Rothay leading onto the A591. I once spotted an otter larking about on the riverside boulders here. Turn right, along the road, and shortly left up the Tarmac lane to Rydal Church. The church was built by Lady Le Fleming, of Rydal Hall, in 1824. Wordsworth worshipped here. As a poet, he thanked Lady Fleming for her munificence in verse. As a curmudgeon, he moaned, amongst other things, that the pews were constricted, making it painful to pray. A precocious 11 year old John Ruskin once attended chapel here in the presence of Wordsworth. His diary records his disappointment that the poet, instead of declaiming loudly, slept throughout the service. Wordsworth's mouth, he wrote, "was quite large enough to let in a sufficient quantity of beef or mutton and to let out a sufficient quantity of poetry".

Carry on up the lane above the church to "Public Footpath" and "Tea Room" signs, above an opening on your right. Rydal Mount, where Wordsworth lived from 1813 to his death in 1850, stands higher up the lane. It's open to visitors, displaying the elegant, comfortable furnishings and fine gardens of Wordsworth's time. Children, however, may be more stimulated by the "Tea Room" sign.

Follow the "Footpath" signs through the buildings of Rydal Hall, crossing a bridge over cascading Rydal Beck. Upon emerging between the last buildings, look right for some steep steps down to a waterfall spilling into a lovely pool. Retrace your steps and follow the pleasant path through Rydal Park, with Todd Crag forming the skyline to your right, to emerge onto the A591 and so back to Ambleside.

Walk 4

Jenkin Crag

Length of walk: 5 miles (To Brockhole 3 miles).
Start/finish: The Low Fold car-park on the A591 (Lake Road) near
Waterhead and virtually opposite the Hayes Garden Centre.
Terrain: Wooded paths to a viewpoint then pleasant "lanes" to
Brockhole Visitor Centre. You could return by motor launch.

First, it would be wise to check if the Brockhole Visitor Centre is open and the times of the launches if you plan to return this way. From the rear of the car-park turn right then shortly left up a Tarmac strip, signposted "Jenkin Crag/Skelghyll/Troutbeck". To your left, looming above the rooftops of Ambleside, like a lumpy, badly-stuffed armchair of fells, is the Fairfield Horseshoe. To its right is Red Screes, with Kirkstone Road snaking up its lower slopes.

At the Strawberry Bank fork keep right, signposted "Jenkin Crag". To your right now, rising above the wooded foothills beyond Windermere like two jostling whales, are Coniston Old Man and Wetherlam. Closer at hand, Todd Crag overlooks Waterhead. At the Broad Ings, "Broad Meadows", fork keep right, signposted "Skelghyll Wood". After entering Skelghyll Wood, Stencher Beck is crossed by a stone bridge, signposted "Jenkin Crag", with a direction arrow, on its parapet. (We once spotted a fox slinking through the trees here.) The path begins to climb alongside the wall to a gap singposted "Jenkin Crag". Turn through the gap and out of the trees onto the slabby summit. Search the far shore of Windermere, below the glinting surface of Blelham Tarn, for the parapets of Wray Castle. This grandiose "folly" was built in 1840 from profits made from gin. Further left are the wooded Claife Heights, haunt of the ghostly Crier of Claife.

Walk back through the gap and climb right to emerge from the trees, to see that a flotilla of wooded islands appear to have jammed together in the Windermere narrows. Now descend through gates into the yard of High Skelghyll Farm. Go through the farmyard and down the Tarmac strip to cross a bridge over the Hol Beck. Continue down the twisting Tarmac, passing Low Skelghyll house. The Tarmac then swings left across the fellside, becomes enclosed as Skelghyll Lane, and climbs a little. If you have children with you and they're complaining a little, remind them of the

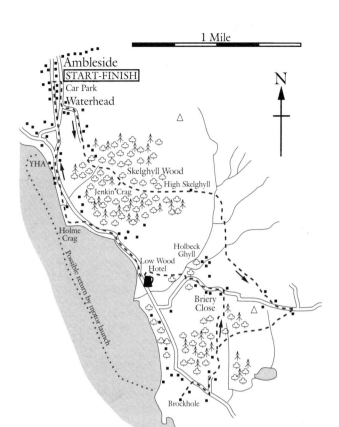

1 Mile

N

pleasures to come at Brockhole and the return in a motor launch.

When Skelghyll Lane joins a minor road, walk left to Castle Syke Farm and a "Public Bridleway" sign. Turn right, and down between buildings. Continue pleasantly down grassy Mirk Lane before going left of extensive buildings to meet a "Private Road. No Right-of-Way" sign. Turn right, to see and follow a "Public Bridleway" sign and waymarker arrows alongside a wall, then left (arrowed) to a gate. Go through the gate and climb Mirk Lane along the fringe of a wood.

The name Mirk Lane and the surroundings may remind Tolkien addicts of Bilbo Baggins' encounter with giant spiders in the labyrinths of the

Mirkwood. Look out for a waymarker (arrowed) stake near a gap in the woods to your right. Ignore it for the moment, but remember it, for if, after visiting Brockhole, you plan to walk rather than sail back to Waterhead, you must return to this point. For the moment carry on, soon to descend, ignoring a path forking right through a gate, and join the Tarmac drive of the Criterion Management Centre. Walk along the Tarmac to the A591 and cross it. Turn right to the entrance to Brockhole Visitor Centre. I haven't the space to go into detail of what Brockhole, "the badgers' hollow", has to offer both adult and child. Sufficient to say it's worth the walk.

Should you decide to walk back to Waterhead, retrace your steps to the way-marker stake in Mirk Lane previously described. Here, turn left and follow a footpath alongside a fence through the woods (watch out for those giant spiders!) to a stile. Cross the stile and continue along the path, swinging left to a stone stile on the edge of the wood. Cross this, and turn right then left up a field path squeezed between fences to emerge onto a minor road.

Turn left down the road, passing the entrance to Briery Close. Charlotte Bronte stayed here in 1850, but found the company irksome and longed "to run away by myself in amongst the hills and dales." After passing the entrance to Holbeck Ghyll Country Restaurant, the road turns left and downhill. A short way down, a "Public Footpath" sign leads you into the woods on your right, then down to and across a footbridge over the Hol Beck and up to a metal gate on the edge of the wood.

Go through the gate and across the field to emerge into the car-park at the rear of the Low Wood Hotel. The view beyond the hotel roof, of the gleaming lake and the array of fells beyond, is breathtaking. From left to right march Coniston Old Man, Wetherlam, Crinkle Crags, Bowfell and the Langdale Pikes. The present hotel was built in 1850 to replace an older inn. Thomas West, in 1778, wrote, "No other inn on this route has so fine a view of the lake". A small cannon was kept at the inn to delight visitors with its echo. Go down between buildings to and across the A591. Turn right along the road for just over half a mile to where roadside arrows indicate a sharp right-hand bend.

Turn down left here across a stile into the National Trust's Jenkin Field. Either walk straight across the field or, rather, follow the shoreline around a rocky point, enjoying the view, the reflections, the play of light upon the water, the sailing boats, perhaps even the water-skiers. Cross the stile at the far end of the field back onto the A591. Turn left to Waterhead and so on past the garden centre to the car-park.

Wansfell Pike

Length of walk: 5 miles.
Start/finish: Troutbeck Church, on the A592 Windermere-Penrith road.
Parking spaces down the side road below the church, on the bank of
Trout Beck, and around the corner of the A592, above the church.
Terrain: Field paths and a shepherds' drove road help you "bag" two
fine tops. Then it's downhill all the way.

Troutbeck Jesus Church is most certainly worth a visit. There have been churches on this site since 1506 and probably even earlier. The lovely east window designed by the "Pre-Raphaelite" artists Burne-Jones, Ford Maddox Brown and William Morris, is just one of the fascinating features. Start by a "Public Bridleway" sign on the A592 just above the church. Parents take note of the nearby children's playground. A promise that they can spend time here, at the end of the walk, might stop those cries of "How much further is it?".

After passing the playground, look for a waymarked (yellow arrow) gate/stile on your right. Beyond this, climb alongside a fence to a gate, and a further gate. Beyond this, another gate leads right onto a wider track. Turn left and follow this to a junction of paths and Tarmac strip, with a signpost above to your left. The Mortal Man, a 17th century inn, with an interesting signboard, dominates the rise ahead. The sign reads:

> *"Thou Mortal Man, who liv'st by bread,*
> *What is it makes thy nose so red?*
> *Thou silly fool, that look'st so pale,*
> *'Tis drinking Sally Birkett's ale!"*

Turn left, "To the Village", keeping your eyes peeled for a "Public Bridleway" sign on your right, partially hidden by a tree. Turn right here and climb a narrow, somewhat overgrown path, to emerge onto a road. Turn left. A "Public Footpath/Nanny Lane" sign above the wall to your left guides you right, around the corner of a

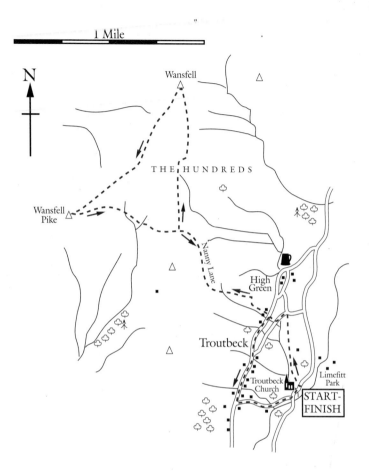

building, to a gate. Beyond the gate, Nanny Lane is steep and stony, but gradually the angle eases and it becomes grassy underfoot. By the time you have passed through a fence and gate/stile, the knobbly ridge of Wansfell, your objective, will loom ahead. To your right, Ill Bell, "the bell-shaped hill" and its humbler partners, Froswick and Yoke, climb above the dalehead.

Nanny Lane eventually swings right near a metal gate, signposted "Footpath to Ambleside, via Wansfell". Ignore this. You will return this way. Continue up Nanny Lane to its end, where a stile (waymarked) climbs the wall to your left. Beyond the stile, climb onto a grassy knoll crowned by a cairn. From here, follow a narrow path, marked by cairns, rightwards across the moor. Glance back for a view of Windermere. A final grassy climb leads to the cairn crowning Wansfell. As you step up to the cairn, the quarry-gutted bulk of Red Screes rises before you. Arrayed to its right, across the gap of Kirkstone Pass, are Stony Cove Pike, Thornthwaite Crag, crowned by its distinctive chimney-like cairn, Froswick, Ill Bell and Yoke.

According to the Ordnance Survey, the path furrowing down the fellside to the left of Froswick is part of the Roman military road from which High Street takes its name. Fairfield's flat top peeks to the left of Red Screes. From it, a long undulating ridge eventually plunges into Rydal Water. Above Rydal Water, spot a dark sliver of Grasmere and, above Grasmere, the Langdale Pikes. Left of the Pikes, look for Bowfell, with Scafell Pike, England's highest peak, looming beyond, then Crinkle Crags, Wrynose Pass, Wetherlam and Coniston Old Man.

Leave the peaceful summit of Wansfell, turning left along the undulating ridge, sometimes on the crest, sometimes alongside the wall coming up from your right, to reach the cairn and stile crowning, probably crowded, Wansfell Pike. The view down Windermere is superb.

Turn left down the good path across the moor to emerge back into Nanny Lane through the metal gate. Descend the lane back to Troutbeck. On reaching the road, turn right, and walk through Troutbeck village, admiring the many lovingly preserved houses and cottages. Many of the houses date back to the 17th century. Interesting features are round chimneys, crow-stepped gables, outside stone staircases, and many have fine interior wood carvings. Like me, I'm sure you would love to own one, should you win the National Lottery of course. Yet in 1864, Eliza Linton wrote of "dirty, neglected Troutbeck – its tumbledown cottages – not one among them straight according to the plumb line – its destitution and penury". Notice the three wells in the wall on your right. Were these a "last filling station" for the poor horses who used to haul coaches over Kirkstone Pass?

At a telephone kiosk on your right, just before the Post Office, turn left down a narrow road, to pass alongside the Trout Beck and reach the A592 just below the church.

Allen Knott

> **Length of walk: 4 miles.**
> **Start/finish: Troutbeck Church, on the A592 Windermere-Penrith road.**
> **Parking spaces down the side road below the church, on the bank of the Trout Beck, and around the corner of the A592, above the church.**
> **Terrain: Pleasant, easy walking on field and wooded paths with a short, optional, climb to a viewpoint.**

Before starting the walk, please read the information regarding Troutbeck Church and the adjacent children's playground given in Walk 5.

From the church, walk down the A592 and across the bridge. Follow the road beyond for a short distance, then cross it to an opening marked by a "Public Bridleway" sign. Climb the stony enclosed path which eventually swings right to pass through a gate. Climb on, to swing left past a gate marked "Private". The path now twists as it climbs, before straightening. Look for an unmarked gate on your right, with a stone stile in the wall alongside it. (There may still be a rusting harrow and other agricultural debris on the verge opposite the gate.)

Go through the gate and climb a faint sunken path, alongside a wall, to a gate near the edge of a wood. Beyond this gate are two waymarker stakes (yellow arrows), the second pointing leftwards. Climb across the field to a stile(waymarked). Cross this and the field beyond to a gap in an old wall where a waymarker arrow points left. (The dwelling to your right is called Longmire. The Longmires lived hereabouts for generations and some lived long. One Margaret Longmire died in 1868 aged 104.)

Follow the arrow, not the obvious path ahead, and climb left alongside the old, tumbled wall to a stone stile (waymarked) leading into Longmire Road. Turn right and follow this rough "road" to its eventual junction with the minor road linking Ings with Troutbeck.

Experts argue that Longmire Road may be the southern end of the Roman Road over High Street and it may have joined a Roman Road that may have linked the Roman fort at Watercrook, near Kendal, with "Galava", the Roman fort at Ambleside. Allen Knott, your next objective, marked by the

Ordnance Survey as a "settlement", may have been the site of a Roman fort guarding this junction. There seems little hard evidence to prove any of this but it all adds interest and romance. It could add to the enjoyment to think you are marching in the steps of Roman legions towards a Roman fort.

At the junction, turn right, signposted "Patterdale via Troutbeck" and down the road to a gate/stile on your left, signposted "Public Footpath/Far Orrest". Follow the path, bending left, to pass through a gap in a walled enclosure (National Trust property), guarding Allen Knott. Walk through the enclosure to a gate. Turn left here and climb alongside the wall onto the rocky summit of Allen Knott (724 feet), site of a Roman or "Ancient Brit" stronghold, no one appears certain. What is certain is the superb view over Windermere - "Vinandr's Water". Analysis of pollen accumulated in the mud and silt of Lakeland tarns suggests that once the fells were forested to nearly two thousand feet. If Brigante warriors or Roman legionaries did stand guard here, how much of this splendour of glimmering lake and high blue fells arrayed across the horizon could they see?

Behind you lies the Troutbeck valley and its guardian fells. From the left, Wansfell, Red Screes, Stony Cove Pike, Thornthwaite Crag, its huge "beacon" a pimple from here, Froswick, Ill Bell and Yoke. If you can identify the Roman Road twisting down the side of Froswick (see Walk 5), you might agree there's a possible link with the Longmire Road and where you stand. Return down to the gate and go through into a narrow, walled path. At its end, turn right through a gate, signposted "Crosses Farm/Windermere", and on down to and through a gate/stile leading left into the hamlet of Far Orrest. Turn right through a gate, signposted "Public Footpath/Troutbeck", and follow the Tarmac strip down to join a minor road.

Turn left, then immediately right, at a "Public Footpath" sign, to go down to a stile in a gap between a barn and a house. Frank Leaver makes stoves, apparently in the barn, an example of his craftsmanship standing amidst a floral display outside it. Before crossing the stile, look down to your right at a poignant memorial to "Higglety-Pigglety 1985-1990". Beyond the stile, a terraced path leads pleasantly down to a gate leading onto the A592. Note the magnificent Scots Pine near the gate.

Cross the road and turn right up the roadside footpath. Follow it over the hill, past a road junction, and down to where a "Public Bridleway" sign points left. Go through the gate and down the field to a gate leading onto footbridges over the Trout Beck. Across these, climb an enclosed path to emerge onto a minor road. Climb right, along the road, to a road junction near Town End, a preserved early 17th century dwelling owned for many generations by the Browne family, and now by the National Trust, and open to visitors. Across the road is Town End Barn, a "bank barn" with an obvious "spinning gallery". By building a two-storey barn into a bank, access was gained to both floors from ground level. Hay stored in the top floor could be fed down to stock on the ground floor. Was a "spinning gallery" a place where wool was spun, or just hung out to dry, or just a storage veranda? Apparently experts can't agree.

Continue along the road into Troutbeck. There are other lovely examples of traditional dwellings over the wall to your right. At the Post Office, turn right down a narrow road to rejoin the A592 near the church.

Walk 7

Loughrigg Tarn

Length of walk: 4 miles.
Start/finish: National Trust "Silverthwaite" car-park, Great Langdale.
From Ambleside, follow the A593 to Skelwith Bridge. Turn right here,
along the B5343 (Langdale) road. After roughly half a mile, look for
an opening on your right, signposted "'P' Walk to Elterwater" and
"National Trust/Silverthwaite". Turn right and park here.
Terrain: A waterfall, a tarn, a peak, all gems, are "bagged" by field and
woodland paths with one steepish, stony ascent and descent.

Leave the car-park, cross the road, go through a gap marked "Elterwater
Langdale" and down to a stile. Cross the stile and follow the path leftwards
to a gate at the edge of woodland. Beyond the gate, a path takes you above
the dark surface of the River Brathay and towards the sound of cascading
water. Shortly, a path leads down to a metal walkway leading out onto slabby
rocks above Skelwith Force. Skelwith means "noisy ford" and Force means
"waterfall". Below, to your left, another walkway leads onto rocky ledges
below the fall. Take due care should the rock be greasy or the fall in spate.

Climb back up to the path by the wall and turn right. Within yards, follow a
path forking left and up onto the Langdale road. Turn right down the road
until opposite a stile and "Public Footpath" sign. Cross the road and the stile
and climb to a gate leading into a narrow, tree-cloistered path. Where this
ends, cross a stone stile to your right and climb a fenced path into the Neaum
Crag holiday-chalet complex. Climb straight ahead up the Tarmac strip
between chalets, keeping your eyes peeled for the guiding yellow
waymarkers (arrows). When the Tarmac and the chalets end the angle eases
and a grassy path leads on into trees.

A stile then leads out into open ground, giving your first glimpse of Loughrigg
looming above the dark, glinting waters of Loughrigg Tarn. Loughrigg means
"ridge above the lake." Follow the path down through the bracken to a minor
road. Turn left along the road, then shortly right over a stile marked "Public
Footpath". Cross the field to a stile. Beyond this, the path forks. For the
moment, ignore the path forking right to the shore of the tarn and climb left to
a gate leading onto a narrow road, near a house. Turn left to shortly see, on

21

your right, a bench with a gate marked "Loughrigg Fell" behind it.

Go through the gate and climb leftwards alongside the wall. Ignore a gap in the wall and climb up to an ill-fitting gate, enabling you to squeeze through it without opening. Just beyond this gate is a cairn with a stile beyond that. Don't cross the stile. Turn right at the cairn and climb the steep, stony path through the bracken above. If you find it hard going, remember, "A view is like bootlaces, it's a good excuse for lots of halts, going up". (Graham Sutton.) Elter Water, "the lake of the swans", is a collection of wooded creeks from here. Great Langdale twists rightwards, between its renowned Pikes and the long, low ridge of Lingmoor, to come to a juddering halt below the mighty flanks of Bowfell. Left of Elter Water, Little Langdale is dominated by Wetherlam, Swirl How and Great Carrs, a "horseshoe" of craggy peaks.

The steep stony path gives way to a steep grassy path. Climb on, "say not the struggle nought availeth", and soon the path levels out to join a well-worn crossing path near a large cairn. Climb left along this to the trig-point crowning the summit of Loughrigg (1,099 feet). Beyond and below lie Grasmere lake and village. The obvious notch in the fells beyond, with a sliver of Thirlmere gleaming above it, is Dunmail Raise, carrying the A591 north to Keswick. Turn and look back down the gleaming miles of Windermere. Way over to the right Esthwaite Water offers a more humble mirror to the sun. There's more, lots more, of the gorgeous patchwork of fell, field and water that is Lakeland, but I'm restricted for space to describe it.

Retrace your steps (towards Windermere), down to the big cairn. Turn right here and retrace your steps down to the cairn by the wall, then left, through the ill-fitting gate, and down to the gate with the bench on the narrow road

beyond. Turn left along the road, which passes a house then curves around and above Loughrigg Tarn to reach stiles over the fence on either side. Cross the right-hand stile to go down and picnic by the shore of the tarn.

To continue, return over this stile and turn right along the road to a gate, near a house. Beyond the gate, turn right along a path, passing "Dillygarth", to join a Tarmac strip. Turn left to a minor road (post box). Turn right, then left at the next junction.

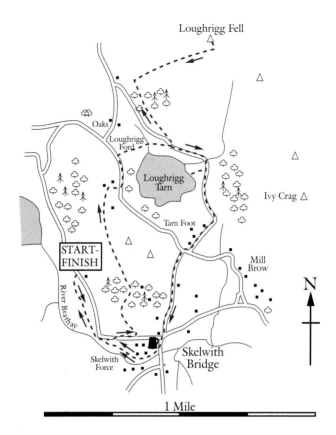

Loughrigg Fell

Oaks

Loughrigg
Ford

Loughrigg
Tarn

Ivy Crag

Tarn Foot

START-
FINISH

Mill
Brow

River Brathay

N

Skelwith
Force

Skelwith
Bridge

1 Mile

Follow this road down to the road junction at Skelwith Bridge. Cross the Langdale road and go along the Coniston road, passing the Skelwith Bridge Hotel, and turn into the Kirkstone Galleries. If you are dying for a pot of tea, or for pop and cake, both wishes could be granted here, plus a browse through a fascinating showroom of wares crafted by traditional Lakeland skills.

On leaving, turn left, and left again at the building's corner ("Footpath" Walk up through the workshops to rejoin the path above Skelwith Force. Continue past the waterfall and through the gate, but please remember, in the field beyond, to follow the path forking right to reach the stile below the car-park.

The Langdale Valley

Length of walk: 4 miles.
Start/finish: The National Trust car-park opposite The Britannia Inn, Elterwater.
Terrain: There is little climbing. Mainly pleasurable walking along field, wooded and riverside paths.

Go out of the car park onto the road and across the bridge spanning the Great Langdale Beck. Turn immediately right, below a "Public Footpath" sign fixed above a "No Through Road" sign. Climb the Tarmac strip, bordered with huge chunks of slate, to a "Footpath" sign on a slate block. Now descend a path, to pass between a wall and a slate spoil-heap.

As you descend, glance across the rocky, foam-flurried beck to the buildings forming the Langdale time-share complex. This was once the site of the Elterwater Gunpowder Mill, which was in production from 1824 to the 1930s. The raw materials, Indian saltpetre and Sicilian sulphur, were initially brought up Windermere by boat and unloaded at a special pier built at Brathay. Most of the powder was used locally for blasting in mines and quarries. When you come to a gap in the wall, go through it and along a faint path to the rim of a frothing waterslide. Scramble left, around a hummock, and along the slate blocks rimming the beck to rejoin the original path through another gap in the wall. Red squirrels can sometimes be seen scurrying back and forth along the top of this wall and leaping into the trees on either side. Squirrels have a long history in Lakeland. They have been depicted on a runic stone found at Bewcastle, on 13th century glass in Bowness, and of course everyone's heard of Squirrel Nutkin!

Turn right, passing two beckside seats, cross the beck by a footbridge and emerge on to the B5343. Walk left, past the Wainwrights Inn (which, I think, refers more to waggon builders than the famed guidebook writer), and follow the road around to the right to shortly see a "Public Footpath" sign on your left. Turn left here and follow a footpath which soon curves right, alongside a wall. When it meets a Tarmac strip, turn left, pass to the right of Thrang Farm, then through a gate into the forecourt of a dwelling called The Thrang. (There are tree swings and an ancient crane to your right here.) Thrang means "narrow passage" and as you walk to the right of the building you will find yourself passing through a gate into a narrow path enclosed by drystone walls. When the enclosing walls bend away turn left, then between walls again, to swing further left onto a stone bridge spanning a deep pool of translucent water. Notice the inscribed stone in the left-hand parapet, "Built 1818 – John and Jane Atkinson". Cross the bridge and turn right along the rough track or scramble up onto the crest of the embankment. The height and strength of the embankment indicates that the tranquil Great Langdale Beck can quickly turn into a raging torrent when snow melts, or thunderstorms rage, in the high fells above.

It is pleasant walking, interspersed with gates, or embankment stiles, with the gill-cleft, crag-pimpled Langdale Pikes rising majestically ahead. Across the meadows to your left are the buildings of Baysbrown Farm (ignore the track leading to them), with craggy, quarry-pocked Lingmoor, "the hill of the ling, or heather", rising beyond.

Eventually, beyond a cattle-grid, the track begins to bear left to reach the buildings of Oak Howe. Walk past the cottage to a somewhat confusing

"Public Footpath" sign with waymarkers pointing ahead and to the right. Turn right, for a few yards, to an obvious path junction, then turn left. The path descends, then climbs up between old walls to a junction with a crossing path (waymarker). Turn left here, along the path climbing across the fellside. When you pass through a gate with a huge slab of rock thrusting out of the ground beyond, look up and over your right shoulder. Imposed upon the skyline is the towering, riven outline of Oak Howe Needle. The path continues through woodland before joining a rough quarry road. Turn left here and down to Baysbrown Farm. Baysbrown translates as "Bruni's Cowshed" and is reputedly the site of one of the earliest homesteads in Langdale.

Pass to the right of the buildings and on to the Tarmac strip, and follow this up into woodland. (I've spotted red squirrels hereabouts too.) When an isolated house is reached, turn down left immediately beyond this by a "Public Bridleway" sign. Virtually within yards, you are transmitted from peaceful woodland into the dusty, racketting heart of a traditional, now

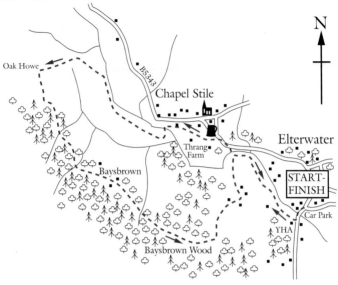

mechanised Lakeland industry. Turn right past the Site Office (waymarker arrow) and on between two huge black corrugated iron sheds. Before turning left and down past the left-hand shed, peer down to your right to see monster lorries, reduced to "Dinky" toys, perched on newly-blasted ledges in the quarry below. A few yards down the road, look out for waymarker arrows on your right, pointing you left, off the road and down the bank into a narrow gap between slate walls. Continue down, passing below a cottage and on through another, higher, walled gap to emerge, once more, on the bank of the Great Langdale Beck.

Turn right, then left through a gap in a wall, then right, along a beckside path, to reach the footbridge you crossed earlier. Turn right here, past the beckside seats, and return to Elterwater by your outward route.

Whorneyside Force

Length of walk: 4¹/₂ miles.
Start/finish: The National Trust car-park near the Old Dungeon Ghyll Hotel, Great Langdale.
Terrain: There's little climbing and it's easy paths except for rougher, less well-trodden ground near the waterfall.

Walk back down the drive and cross the Tarmac to a gate. Go through the gate and slant left across the field to a gate leading onto a packhorse bridge over the Great Langdale Beck. Cross the bridge and turn right through a gate, signposted "Public Footpath/Oxendale/The Band", and follow the Tarmac strip through the fields to Stool End Farm.

The bulky ridge rising ahead is The Band, which divides Oxendale, on the left, from Mickleden, "the big valley". Towering above Oxendale, their craggy slopes split by the shadowy cleft of Crinkle Gill, are Crinkle Crags, in Old English "cringol", meaning wrinkled or twisted. Left of Crinkle Crags and thrusting closer are the rocky slopes of Pike O'Blisco.

The towering spire of rock to your right is Pike O'Stickle, "peak with a sharp summit". Edward Baines, climbing it in 1829, wrote, "The view down Langdale is enough to make a person of good nerves tremble, though the top is not so sharp as it seems from a distance". Today, we fellwalkers climb it in our scores, and squat on its top, phlegmatically munching our butties and slurping our tea but still thrilling to the sense of space and mountains arrayed around us. The pale scree-chute slashing down the fellside below it is Stone Axe Gully, where, in 1947, a Neolithic "stone axe factory" was discovered, by chance, in a shallow cave half way down it. Rough axes were transported from this factory, and others since discovered, to the coastal sands for polishing, then distributed throughout Britain, where many have since surfaced.

At Stool End Farm, go through the farmyard and out onto the fellside through a gate marked "Footpath"

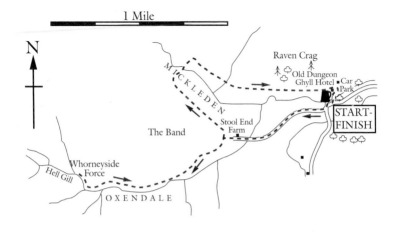

away to the left of the farmhouse. Set in the ground beyond the gate are two slate signposts "Path to The Band/Path to Mickleden". Climb left, alongside the wall, passing where The Band path forks right, then continue down and through the waymarked (arrowed) gate leading into Oxendale. Follow the path beyond to a stone sheepfold which is entered by a waymarked gate. Beyond the sheepfold, a footbridge on your left crosses the Oxendale Beck. Ignore this and continue up the valley.

The path beyond that footbridge climbs to Red Tarn, lying, at 1850 feet, between Pike O'Blisco and Cold Pike. Analysis of pollen accumulated in the mud and silt of this tarn concluded that the forest once reached up to its shores. So you can see why Neolithic Lakeland man needed to craft axes to clear the woodland for space to live and farm. Modern experiments have shown that stone axes were very effective, and they must have been skilled field geologists in picking out outcrops suitable for axe making.

When the wall on your right turns uphill, you have a choice of two paths. You can either continue ahead along a path which clings to the very edge of the steepening banks of the beck, with one slightly awkward crossing of a rocky tributary beck; or, climb right, to shortly swing left along an easier path through the bracken higher up the fellside. Both paths merge at the footbridge over Hell Gill.

Upon the footbridge, you are near the confluence of Browney Gill, furthest left, Crinkle Gill, and Hell Gill, which flows under you. It's a wild, rugged scene and a noisy one should the gills be in spate. To climb the rocky beds of such gills is known as "becking". Once "becking" with a friend, a hold came away in my hand and I crash-dived into a deep pool, big boots, rucksack, hearing aid and all. I thought I was never going to come up! When I did eventually surface it was to find my companion hysterical with laughter. To my surprise, my hearing aid recovered after several days of squawking and hissing indignantly.

To reach the foot of Whorneyside Force, which you can partially see to your right around a curve in Hell Gill, cross the bridge and turn immediately right along a faint path on the left bank of Hell Gill. This path crosses some rough and shaley ground, but without danger, to reach the small cascades below the main fall. It's possible to get closer to the foot of the fall by crossing a scree-chute and making a couple of strides above a steep bank. If you are not wearing boots, however, and it's greasy, be very careful for you have to return. If the beck is not in spate, it's easy to boulder-hop across to the far bank from where you might find it easier to get to the pool at the foot of the fall.

Retrace your steps to the footbridge and back down to the rear of Stool End Farm. Don't go through the "Footpath" gate. Turn left, behind the farmhouse, following the "Path to Mickleden" sign at your feet. Walk alongside a wall to a gate. Beyond the gate, turn right then left between walls. When the walls turn away follow the path veering right to a footbridge over the Mickleden Beck below a weir. It's a bonny spot for a picnic. Bare and bleak Mickleden is a classic U-shaped valley, scooped out by a glacier when the ice-cap that covered Lakeland's fells melted. The debris it left behind lies under the cluster of drumlins dimpling the dalehead.

Cross the bridge and follow the path alongside a wall to join a wider, stonier crossing path near a wall corner. Turn right along this path. As you walk, look over the fields to your right to see the road zig-zagging over to Little Langdale, with Side Pike and Lingmoor rising above. Continue to a stile at the rear of the hotel leading on to the car-park.

Lingmoor

Length of walk: 3¹/₂ miles.
**Start/finish: Drive past the Old Dungeon Ghyll Hotel, Great Langdale,
and on up the hairpins that lead over to Little Langdale. The car-park
is in a small plantation on the left, just past solitary Bleatarn House.
Terrain: The book's rockiest and, optionally, most adventurous walk.**

Leave the car park and turn right up the road. When it begins to drop towards
Bleatarn House, turn right up a steepish path climbing the right bank of a
gill. If you find it a "slog", the view behind you is a good excuse to stop. The
Langdale Pikes, towering above the craggy cone of Side Pike, dominate.
Bow Fell, 500 feet higher and the king of Langdale's mountains, stands back
and you only get a taste of the mighty rampart it forms, with Crinkle Crags,
around the dalehead. Below you gleams Blea Tarn, "the dark tarn". Tarn is
derived from the Old Norse word "tjorn", meaning tear. The tarns were the
"tears of the mountains" to Lakeland's Norsemen, which proves that some
Vikings were poets rather than pillagers like Ragnar of the Hairy Breeks and
his pungent sidekicks. To your left, beyond the head of Little Langdale, rise
Wetherlam, Swirl How and Great Carrs.

When a wall is glimpsed ahead, the path slants left, through some splendid
pines, into the head of the gill to a fence/stile in a gap in the wall. Cross the
fence and climb steeply left alongside the wall to a stile in a crossing fence
near the cairn crowning the summit of Lingmoor (1538 feet), "the fell of the
ling, or heather". The 2¹/₂" OS map says "Brown Howe" but Wainwright,
Griffin, a million fellwalkers, and me, call it "Lingmoor". Windermere is
now added to the view, and for the collector of scenic curiosities, given a
clear day, Blackpool Tower may be picked out to the left of Wetherlam.

Follow the path beyond the cairn, alongside the wall/fence crowning the ridge,
the Langdale Pikes looking more magnificent with every onward step. Ruskin
judged the Pikes "the loveliest rock-scenery, chased with silver waterfalls, I
ever set foot or heart upon". Below, to your right, lies rarely visited Lingmoor
Tarn, its surface a thick pink and white carpet in May when the lovely
Bogbean flowers. There's one slabby outcrop, just above a crossing wall,
which should be descended carefully if the rock is greasy. Below this, climb
left over a stile, then right, down the ridge with the wall now on your right.

Lakeland's network of drystone walls, "running like live things about the fells", (Hugh Walpole), was largely built between 1750 and 1850. It was the work of wallers who often camped on the high fells for days at a time, in all weathers and for a pittance. In 1845 walls cost 8 shillings per rood (seven yards), including the cost of carting and gathering. In 1969 it was 200 times as much. When you reach the stile in the fence below rather forbidding-looking Side Pike you have the choice of an adventurous option or an easy option.

The "Fat Man's Agony" Option: Cross the stile and climb the path which goes right, then left and down and round to a ledge apparently blocked by a rock pinnacle. Pushing your rucksack before you, squeeze behind the pinnacle onto the ledge beyond. It's good fun and much easier than it looks. I've encouraged several dubious and "pleasantly plump" ladies and gentlemen safely through. Ancient guidebooks used to call such features a "Fat Man's Agony". Children will love it and probably want to go back and forth time and again – just keep your eye on them. Carefully follow the ledge beyond the pinnacle around a corner to where the path forks. Turn right here and follow the path climbing diagonally across the fellside to join a crossing path near an old wall. Turn right up this path to shortly reach the summit of Side Pike (1187 feet). Don't let children roam around here, for there are crags below.

To descend, return down the path alongside the old wall into a dip, then slightly up again onto the crest of a rocky step crowned by a cairn (pile of stones), to your left. Below, you will see the high point of the hairpin road you drove over, your next objective. Scramble down the rocky step then step over the wall on your right to another cairn. Walk right from this cairn, following a path marked with cairns, (so watch for them), zig-zagging down grass broken with rocky steps. It may seem that you are heading into Great Langdale but at a cairn perched above a grassy path dropping left, the road

C.M. Isherwood

31

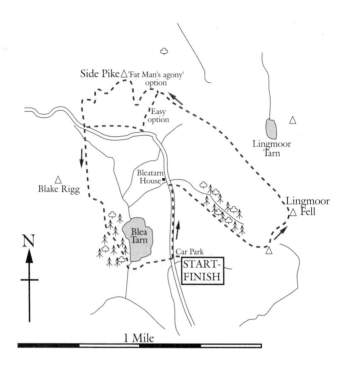

Side Pike △ 'Fat Man's agony'
option

'Easy
option

Lingmoor
Tarn

△

Bleatarn
House

△ Lingmoor
Fell

Blake Rigg
△

Blea
Tarn

Car Park
START-
FINISH

△

N

1 Mile

you're aiming for comes into view to your left and close. Drop down to the grassy path and descend it left to pass an old sheepfold and a stone memorial seat before crossing a stile onto the road. The Easy Option: Don't cross the stile in the fence below Side Pike. Turn left and descend the path to a stile lower down in the fence. Cross this and follow a path through the bracken, across the fellside above the road, to a gap in a wall. Go through the gap, then turn left past a stone memorial seat and cross a stile onto the road.

Whichever option you've taken, now cross the road, go left through a gap in a wall and follow the worn path down towards Blea Tarn. A tunnel of rhododendrons leads you along the western shore before you turn left over a footbridge and through a gate onto the grassy southern shore, with its superb view, real and reflected, of the Langdale Pikes. Look up with pride at the rugged skyline you have traversed. In the film "She'll Be Wearing Pink Pyjamas" Julie Walters and friends skinny-dipped here. With the car-park nearby it's a very popular spot, so if you're thinking of emulating them make sure you've got your "cossy". Continue along the path to the car-park.